salmonpoetry

*Celebrating 35 Years
of Literary Publishing*

Sometimes I Hear the Clock Speak

LORI DESROSIERS

8·11·17

To Tim,

Thank you with all my heart
for the excellent experience in
workshop at fAWC.

Lori Desrosiers

Published in 2016 by
Salmon Poetry
Cliffs of Moher, County Clare, Ireland
Website: www.salmonpoetry.com
Email: info@salmonpoetry.com

Copyright © Lori Desrosiers, 2016

ISBN 978-1-910669-30-3

COVER IMAGE: © Olejnik | Dreamstime.com
COVER DESIGN & TYPESETTING: Siobhán Hutson
Printed in Ireland by Sprint Print

Dedicated with love to my mother Blanche,
who gave me her voice.

To my amazing daughters Margot and Gabrielle,
who have brought our voices forward,
for your love and encouragement.

Love and thanks to my husband Gary, who never
complains when I run off to poetry events, and who
makes our house a peaceful place to come home to.

Also much love and thanks to my wonderful friends and
critique group members who helped bring this book to life.

Acknowledgements

The author expresses thanks to the editors of the following, in which some of the poems from this collection first appeared:

Contemporary American Voices: "The Balance Stone", The Bar Where the Physicists Drink", "Guitars" and "Sometimes I Hear the Clock Speak"

String Poet (inaugural issue): "Anniversary"
Inner Sky (chapbook): "Anniversary"

New Verse News: "Sandbar Piano" and "Day after the End of the World"

Inner Sky: "Airless", "Divorce Rondelet" and "New Season"

Blue Fifth Review: "Bee Dancer"

Contents

Skates and Stones

The Balance Stone

after a sculpture of the same name by Isamu Noguchi

there used to be another stone
the ghost stone is not there
above the stone that is

the stone that is is on the roof
of the building where air passes
through windows that are not there

like the quartz gathered in the woods
near the house a child used to live in
who used to be me

the ghost of the child
is balanced on the roof
of what I have forgotten

Before Woodstock

Sitting cross-legged on Mel's shag rug,
Cream on the record player, incense
on the sill, glass bong passed
between friends, smoke rises white, melds
with the music; guitar solos and drums
almost psychedelic, before acid trails.

We were fourteen. Woodstock still ahead
of us, that summer when my mother said no,
but Mel went with other friends,
came back different, drug-savvy,
hanging with the older kids.
A boyfriend gave her Heroin;
rehab instead of college.

But all that would be later. This day
was ours, a safe fog of mind and music
wafted overhead, pre-adolescent, pre-blitz,
newly graduated from *The Monkees*,
crushes on Davy Jones, Sajid Khan.

Weaving headbands on small looms,
rings, bracelets from hemp and beads,
embroidering our jeans, sewing patches,
talking about boys we didn't sleep with.

The summer of Woodstock, I went to camp.
Rick spent all summer trying to get me
to go all the way, but I said no, I wasn't ready,
so he dumped me.

Giggles rise, ropes of smoke,
sun peeks through flower-curtained windows;
her parents think we're playing.

The Year of Bad Decisions

My brother's trombone spit welling up inside,
brass instrument smelled like dirty metal,
unlike my violin, the odor of hardwood,
rosin and horsehair more tactile than gross.

We'd practice in our rooms upstairs,
his bleating drowned out my high notes.
Mother begged us to take breaks,
tempted us with plates of Ritz and cheddar,

a bribe to soothe her delicate ears, knowing
full well we would start again next day.
Perhaps we were the reason she spent so much
time out of the house, finding excuses to leave

us alone for hours on end, we didn't know
her newly single life or what she did at night.
Found out later she was dating the chorus teacher,
whose classroom both my brother and I attended.

Thank goodness she turned down his proposal,
since my brother hated him with a passion,
I don't remember why.
He was a bit of an ass, thinking on it now.

Senior year I played second chair first violins.
then made my way through college, the violin did not.
My brother put aside the trombone, took up guitar,
a fine choice, less spit. We never looked back.

What I Want

To kick some seaweed around,
throw a flat stone into a tide pool,
make it skip four, five, ten times.

To be back in Menemsha summer
with my mother and brother, to be eight
years old and the big sister holding my

brother's hand on the jetty as we stepped from
one rock to another, keeping him away
from slippery places, showing him the

dead man's float, how to use a kickboard.
Once I put a towel on his head to make him
a girl while I sang "Alice, where are you going?'

He sang "Blub, blub, blub" at the end,
I played the piano. He had curls then,
light brown, almost blond. He's balding now.

Want to call but I know he'll just tell
the same stories of how he was
the best singer in our High School

or he won't answer the phone.
Now that we haven't been close for years,
I wonder what *he* wants.

Listening to Beethoven Quartets
(Variations on a Theme)

I am the first violin I send my music aloft
　　I am the second violin I pick up the tune
　　　　I am a cello I echo the notes but deeper
　　　　　　I am a viola I play with the melody and turn it back around

now it laughs at you it laughs at itself
　　now it laughs at you it laughs at me also
　　　　no I don't want to laugh no I don't want to
　　　　　　I will laugh with you and make light of it all

find me in the land of sighs and follow
　　find you in the land of sails and hollow
　　　　oh find me find me find me find me
　　　　　　I have found you, you have found me

you are a dream I sing a high and tender kiss
　　you are a kiss I sing a high and tender dream
　　　　dream with me dream with me we will dream
　　　　　　kiss me kiss him too oh kiss everyone tonight

staccato flight of buzzing bees and lawn chairs
　　buzzing flight of staccato bees and dawn chairs
　　　　bears in chairs bears in chairs
　　　　　　they will not bite they will not bite you now

we will end this soon but you will be
　　you will be surprised at how it will end
　　　　surprise, sing, dance and slide
　　　　　　does it end or does it come back around?

I am the first violin I send my melody
　　I am the second violin I pick up the tune
　　　　I am the cello I echo the notes but deeper
　　　　　　I am the viola I turn it back around

Sandbar Piano

MIAMI (AP) – A grand piano
recently showed up on a sandbar
in Miami's Biscayne Bay, about
200 yards from condominiums
on the shore.

Perhaps jellyfish
will learn to play
Bach Cantatas,
or old Diver Dan's composition:
Seaweed Suite in C minor,
for squid trumpet, piano
and four octopus orchestra.

It's Hard to be Six

I tell my mother the truth.
She never believes me.
One night I fly around the living room ceiling
watch my parents and their guests dancing,
playing the piano and drinking whiskey.
I tell her I can fly.
You can't fly. It was a dream says my mother.
She locks the windows.

I tell my parents my baby brother can talk.
They never believe me.
Playing upstairs, I say to him
make the teddy bear say *I'm going to school*
My brother says, *I'm going to school.*
He says whatever I tell him.
When they put him in the high chair
and he wants something,
all he has to do is point and say Umm
and they jump to get it.

I see a big black snake in the living room.
I run to tell my mother.
She says, *Sure there is, honey.*
She never believes me.
I take her hand and show her.
She screams, grabs me,
runs into the bedroom.
Later, my father and the policeman
show the snake the way out.
It's hard to be six.

Skate Pond, 1962 (Age 7)

Skating alone, someone grabs my hand
and pulls.
I almost fall. It is the end
of the terrible formation called a whip.

Ten or twenty big kids
holding hands, going much too fast for me.
I tumble and am dragged along, until they let me go.

I limp across the ice, all skate strings and bloody knees.
Nobody comes to check.
Nobody cares.

Dancing with Mother

On the living room's slate floor,
my brother and I twirled while
Mother shimmied to "Never on a Sunday,"
did the Charleston to Elvis records

pulled from the pile of 45s on the shelf,
the needle delicately placed, skimming
vinyl grooves on wooden console.

Mother in her skirts and slippers,
we'd follow her movements,
slide, step forward, step back, turn.

Mother, now 92, closes her eyes, puts her head back.
Remember when we used to dance in the living room?
I could have been a dancer, you know.

My Violin

has been tucked in the closet for years,
black case, green plush interior, bridge broken,
strings gone, hairless bow on a hook.

Long gone are days of before-school orchestra,
after-school lessons, brown mark under my chin.
Took up guitar, forgot the violin.

You can't sing with a violin,
and no talent, so I thought.
Years later, a friend's violin sitting out

Scheherazade on the music stand,
asked if I could try, it was one we played.
So shocked I almost dropped the instrument.

She explained it was the violin.
If only I had known,
all those years in High School

when I sounded worse than
everyone else, no matter
how hard I practiced.

It was my student violin
that lacked resonance, not I.

Ashkenazy

My mother used to say to me,
Don't tell people you are Jewish.

Fear of others in the shadow
of extermination, of being taken,
everything taken.

We danced the Horah at weddings.
Twice a year we went to Temple;
Rosh Hashanah to hear the cantors,

on Yom Kippur,
the Kol Nidre's mournful song

My people are removed from the ancestors
scattered from Odessa to Philadelphia to California.

Before that —
we forget.

Our tongues echo
a smattering of Yiddish,
a few Russian words.

The voice of the great grandfather
who was a cantor,
whose name we don't know,

rings in my brother's baritone;
the same voice as our grandfather,
who had no time to sing.

Lament

– To my cousins Eileen and Melissa

You welcomed me in Philadelphia
with wide arms and sad smiles.
We stood for your father at graveside,
shoveled earth onto his coffin,
sang the Kaddish, secretly hoping for eternity.
After, we ate kippered salmon and lox,
remembering fried matzo breakfasts,
his stories and sharp wit, his love of horses.
Watched Nick the shih tzu bark at the television.
Took out an old album.
There we stood as teens in mini dresses.
Young parents, Albert, Uncle Sol who died at 58,
their sister Blanche (my mother),
younger than we are now by many years,
her perfect legs, hair and moon face,
smiling and waving from the past.

Yellow Dragonfly

After you met me in the park
we sang Leonard Cohen's

"Dance Me to the End of Love"
on the steps by the church.

I played my samba for you,
with the scat in it, *bada daba daa.*

After your car pulled away,
I walked down the municipal building

steps, swinging my guitar.
A yellow four-winged dragonfly

hovered above my car,
buzzed by the window

as if it had never seen a girl
as if I had never seen a yellow dragonfly.

Echoes and Voices

My Brother's Voice

His speaking voice exactly
like our father's,
but not when he sings.

Dad would try to sing
loudly, out of tune, the *Marseillaise*
running into the ocean.

When he was seven
before antibiotics
they removed his right eardrum.

My brother sings
more like my grandfather
on our mother's side

who sang Russian songs
and snippets of operas
as he cooked fried matzo.

When my brother was in school
the girls would come to listen
to auditions for his chorus solos.

He still sings quite well,
but the schoolgirls have forgotten him,
and he has no one to cook for.

Reveille

7:15am at YMCA camp
in New Hampshire.
They sometimes played it jazzy.
Dun, dun, da, da, dun.
I heard a bugle in my head
every morning, all year.
Didn't need an alarm for school,
always made it to orchestra by eight,
all through high school
four years of camp stuck hard.
At night I heard Taps.

Daughter's Voice

Even in the nursery
at the hospital
I could tell
my daughter Margot
from the other babies
by her singing.
Well, it wasn't singing yet
but she cried a pretty cry
it was tuneful
and since I am a singer
and so was my mother
and grandmother,
this didn't surprise me,
but it moved me
how she was bringing
the generations forward.
And now, when I hear her sing,
I am still taken
by our mothers
in her voice.

Sestina for my Daughter Margot

You play guitar with either hand,
thanked me for your voice, my voice.
First child, I learned so late
to parent, you were already gone.
I've missed you since you left,
so young to be on your own.

Back in the house we used to own,
in New York you used to hold my hand.
We'd take long walks before your father left,
to let him rest, avoid his angry voice.
Eight years of running before he was gone.
Ten years I tried, but it was just too late.

Amazing now, our closeness of late.
You call me often on your own.
My lovely girl, you seem less gone.
You visit me and hold my hand,
I bask in the timbre of your voice.
Time helps forget the pain we left.

For a time you and I were left.
We played together, slept late,
I learned to fix things, found new voice,
figured out our future on our own,
slowly stilled my trembling hand.
Years went by before the fear was gone.

I turned around, blinked and you were gone.
Just fourteen years of memories were left.
Away at school, I could not hold your hand.
How could I know if you had stayed up late?
Your teachers were your parents, not your own.
Vacations seemed we had less closeness left.

You sang at school, I could not hear your voice.
It was my fault that you were gone.
Too weak or dumb to stay strong on my own,
married again, five years, then left.
Finally found myself, almost too late.
Thank you for taking back my hand.

On your CD, I listen to your voice,
songs written by your hand, no longer gone.
Your whole life still ahead, it's not too late.

Travis and Other Picks

Took up guitar on the wide lawn at camp
between the corn field and the barn
where the theater kids hung their feet
from the loft where the lights were kept.

Played my first five chords and learned
Travis, Arpeggio and other picks.
Practiced smoking cigarettes and kept a boy
at bay until he dumped me for an easier girl.

Wrote my first song about finding love
which wouldn't happen that summer.
Acted in a Tennessee Williams play.
The director told me I couldn't act.

Went to hear Santana at Tanglewood
where I smoked a whole pack of Tarrytons
and threw up in the bathroom.
Almost missed the final set, it was amazing.

We learned songs by Buffy Saint Marie,
Judy Collins, Joan Baez, James Taylor
practiced the chords, the picks, the riffs,
thinking one day we'd be famous too.

That summer we didn't go to Woodstock.
Our parents sent us to camp instead,
thinking we'd be better off in Stockbridge.

First Margot

Margot hated her name.
She was my violin teacher
from age six to the end of High School.
I tried to talk to her sometimes,
but mostly she made me practice.

She wanted me to learn viola too,
but I had a hard time with the violin.
so thought I had no talent
and she didn't disagree with me;
perhaps we never had the conversation.

I named my first daughter Margot,
because at the time, Margot
seemed like the prettiest name,
and I had pretty much forgotten
this woman who hated her name.

My Father's Ear

At age seven my father went half deaf.
His right ear succumbed to an infection,
before antibiotics.
He asked us to sit on his left side,
his patients too.
He mourned that ear because he loved music;
Beethoven, Mozart, the classics gave him joy.
He sang along loudly, conducted in the air,
found headphones he could turn up on one side.
Music still brings him back to me.

Listening to my son-in-law sing in Greek

He looks at my daughter
while he sings,
plays the bouzouki
as if she were the inspiration
for his compositions.

Fingering her guitar,
she laughs.
They sing and play together;
who is whose muse
is not important.

Dancing with Valerie

Eighth grade.
Valerie Clark and I
danced to Motown
in her mother's kitchen,
while down in Washington
marchers listened to Dr. King.
Valerie and I didn't notice
the colors of our skin.

I still dance like a black girl.
We wanted to form a group.
Thought we'd be famous someday,
then she moved away.

Late Spring

Another April has faded and gone
plum blossoms turned to ruby leaf
the forsythia's yellow now green
my tulips never came up this year
perhaps rabbits got them again
and we missed the sudden rush
of cedar waxwings.

The cranberry is now bare of berries
dogwoods cradle their white crosses
the lilies are waiting for rain
a million baby maples dot the lawn
soon to be surprised at a first mowing
and children blow white dandelion seeds
in the low vernal tilt of sunlight

Tulip Tree

under tulip tree at the top of a hill
a girl grew long and sinewy
like the vines that tried to climb
the ancient tree to no avail
but she reached the lowest branches
easily and climbed up high
where she could see the river
and the rooftops below
she knew the name of each tree
which flowers came in spring
which fruit in summer
her bare feet grabbed the earth
walked easily amidst the grass
and rocks her hands touched
each tree as she played
it was a perfect haven
until they moved away
in the city trees were small
and weak their roots bound
small circles in pavement
branches too symmetrical
even old trees in the park
seemed to breathe in short gasps
the dirty air while pigeons coughed
among the spindly branches

Songs and Seasons

Cape Music

The sounds at the beach are unlike those at home.
At home, the television or the radio is always on,
the neighbor's mower is buzzing, or yours.
We are seldom doing the same thing at the
same time, you on your phone, I on my computer.

We sit on the beach, watch cormorants skim and dive,
healthy gulls, fat and well-preened, don't fight over food,
like the gulls do at the shopping mall at home
who have never seen the sea.

Here we are silent, watch sailboats, other
people walking dogs or strolling hand in hand.
We listen to water lap on this
windless day, the chirp and coo of plovers.

We hold hands, watch the sun change from yellow to orange,
the rays transform water into a mirror of sky.
I remember you now.

Guitars

I believe in strum and riff,
in the medley of pluck and thrum
in strings pulled taut to tune
finessed with finger picks,
or tickled with steel for a slide,
in the brrring of a chord,
the vibration of hammer on.

I believe in a good Fake Book.
At the midnight jam
I'll bring my axe, you bring yours.

We'll play St. James Infirmary
and Uncle John's Band
until the sun comes up
over the Hudson or the O-hi-o.

Bee Dancer

(inspired by a collage by Karen Randall)

Her bee wings thrum
nasal noises, thin and reedy,
vibrate in a treble song.

Her world is crimson suede curtains
laid on walls of white stretched canvas
creases folded, lined with brown ribbon.

Carefully placed circle of silk,
round as earth, azure as arctic ice.
Stomps her long black feet.
Dark figure cuts a temper dance.

There is no honey.
This hive is fabric, oil, glue
a nest for apian dancers,
tapping on the gallery floor.

spring again

somnolent blossoms
die every winter rebirth

in spring to fill our yard
and the neighbors' with

the ringing of leaf & petal
the smell of dirt & essence

each year smells
more pungent than the last

Transit of Venus

The sun shakes
on telescopic feed
from Mauna Loa's slope
11,000 feet up.

Three telescopes, three gasses:
hydrogen alpha
white light view, solar filtered
and calcium
change the Sun
from beige to red to blue.

Venus looks quiet
a slow motion creeper
but she is hurtling through space
past the Earth, across Sun's path
barely time to say hello to us
in her oblong orbit.

Today, we track her path,
a black spot on our life star,
Tomorrow, Venus will blink
at us from her regular place
in twilight's darkening sky.

The Spruce Out Back

The wind shakes down a couple
pinecones from the Norway Spruce
someone planted out back
a hundred years ago
for a windbreak.

She is the tallest
in the neighborhood,
and her children thrive
down the block on all sides.

From bird's-eye view
you and I are hidden
below the tree, below roof,
second floor ceiling.

When snow came in October
we lost the dogwood you planted
in front and several pines,
but the spruce just shrugged it off.

These last fifteen years
we sit in the yard in summer
and the grass beneath the spruce
is greener than anywhere
I have loved before.

Compost Mother

I sit in my backyard
watch the flowers die
and I am worried.
When my mother dies
will she be here
part of the earth
like the flowers
a compost mother
to put in the soil
beneath the roses
or like a fish
beneath a corn stalk
a boost of oxygen
her bones pushing
plants to rich harvest
washed clean with rain
burned in the autumn
with the leaves
to make a new mulch
and plant again?

Anniversary

Fifteen years ago
we stood before sunflowers
pushing their seedy faces
up the shed's outer wall,
our feet immersed in
dandelion clover.

Pledged from this day forward
to plant bulbs in Spring,
tulips, daylilies and irises;
push marigold and daisy seeds
into black Summer soil;
build towers for tomatoes,
grids for zucchini, cucumber, peas.

Vowed to sit in Adirondack chairs,
watch cedar waxwings
devour the juniper berries;
to hang thistle for goldfinch,
suet for woodpeckers
from blue spruce branches.

Today, we take the bulbs
from their dark winter storage
beneath the spades and rakes,
gently place them
beneath the ground,
another year, as promised.

Rookery

in april before spring's buds have a chance to push
their leaves through we float on early red blossoms

your legs strain as you paddle the air is crisp dry
our breath rises in white ropes we tug the boat

over mud islands between flooded meadows
soon the sound of what we have been looking for

blue heron large as pterodactyl their nests precarious
on spindly top branches nothing but twigs and mud

even the rise of a camera starts them to flight
a wingspan wider than the length of our kayak

stick feet dangle beneath dinosaur feathers
not a sound but the thwap and rustle of wing

Divorce Rondelet

Break up, break down.
She tried to stay until the end.
Break up break down.
She closeted the wedding gown.
There's only so far one can bend
and only so much love to spend.
Break up, break down.

Oh, Baby, Baby

You are the music I love
golden soul infused with blue
of trumpet and guitar
your rhythms sway me
your beats move my feet
my hips push and push
wilder, wilder you say
shimmy those shoulders
find that slide in your step
your arm around my waist
your other hand resting
where it feels reeal good
and we dance.

What the Clock Said

Reverie Obscura

I am on a bus,
the mountain road, precipitous,
a silver bridge stretches over
churning water below, no railings.
The bus stops, we get out.
I am with a man, perhaps a lover.

The water is gone, now
there is a desert below,
cactus in bloom, green lizards skitter.
I can see for miles.
Sky painting dissolves to fuscia.

Then we are on a train, going backwards.
The world goes by upside down,
a camera obscura, light peeks
through pinhole windows
reflecting on black walls.

We sit upside down
to see the world right side up.
"This is poetry," he says,
and I am falling now,
falling out of the poem.

Airless

A few diehard physicists pointed out that wings are
of no propulsive help in airless void

    – Robert Silverberg, *Earth is the Strangest Planet*

you rendered me airless
in the 1980's when the airwaves
carried new wave music
Elvis Costello and Sting
an outrush of breath
all that pumped-up love
ten years and two babies worth
blown away in one storm
the resulting flight
yours instead of ours
winged your way to the city
where crowds compete for air
and weak trees suspire badly
I aired out the house
unpacked my long-tucked wings
and slowly relearned to breathe

The Bar Where the Physicists Drink

Is a simple old place that serves Guinness.
They sip in sync with the universe,
calculate the time it takes
for heads to dissolve into golden lager,
observe the centrifugal force
of barstool turns, the trigonometry
of dart throws, comment on
the waitress; whether she exists
in time and space while she is on break,
the centripetal force of her inert body
leaning against the outside wall,
inhaling molecules of smoke; debating
if her curvature is equal to her curves.
They don't order martinis, but if they did,
they might contemplate Pascal's 2nd Law
of Hydrostatics, how an olive
affects a change of pressure in a
homogenous, incompressible fluid.
They drink their beers, join the flow of charge
as the current of money quickly ebbs.
When the conjugate quantity of beer consumed
is equivalent to the linear movement of time wasted,
they declare this system closed and depart,
leaving a sense of relative uncertainty at every table.

Library: At the End of the Universe

By the time she got into the library
her backpack was soaked from the pouring rain,
her gloves made her hands feel like icicles,
her toes were curled over to warm themselves.

By the time she had opened her science text,
the formulas danced in their paragraphs,
the light played a game with her spectacles,
her brain was a panel on overload.

By the light of her digital timepiece,
she knew she was tardy for chemistry,
the chemicals bled from her tear ducts,
an audible sigh made some heads turn.

By the scroll of the big screen bulletin
proclaiming the end of the universe,
the students had melted like icicles,
their cell phones blinked blue in the darkness.

The day after the end of the world

I will walk out on my front porch,
watch the children throw snowballs,
cheer on the postman in his high boots,
marvel at sun filtering through pine branches,
sing a song my mother used to sing,
shovel some snow, sweep up the house,
make a call or two, joke about the weather,
pick up an ornament from the floor,
put on the tea kettle, start chicken soup,
sit in my chair, pet the orange cat,
finish the dishes, make the bed,
put in a load of sheets, edit a poem,
remark to my husband
how delightful it is
that we are still here,
after all that hullabaloo.

Film Noir

"Wanda, Wanda," he cries nightly
remembering her azure eyes fading
into black, a camera glamour girl
feathered like a gull, while he
lugged her suitcase up four floors,
stair dwellers staring up her short skirt
slamming doors in shame, frustration,
her way strewn with worry, wishes.
He wonders when all that time fell,
just fell beneath his feet.

The Sunset

tasted like
a plan she made
as yellow melted
like wax petals
and the smell
was broad,
textured
and burned
like thunder.

New Season

I am alive,
running over rocks,
wet, still tipped with
winter's frosting,
almost slip,
barely holding on.
This is the key
to spring's return
along garden path,
already blooming
with forsythia, cherry.
Soon, marigolds
will ring tomatoes,
peppers, squash,
leaving winter
a bookmark
in memory.

Descent

The two of us started
down the steps
the unending steps
to the beach below
holding grey rails
dizzy with height
we forgot the view
stopped at each platform
repositioned our hold
on canvas and metal chairs
cutting into armpits
slipped but didn't fall
seemed a long journey.
Finally the sand
singed our footprints.
We laid out a blanket
unfolded the chairs
positioned a picnic
sank into our seats
breathed in the sun
looked to the horizon
took a double take
pointed, shouted,
whale spouts, then
a fin, a tail, a shiny slick
left by a humpback
a tribute to our descent.

Stuck Bee

My friend's bees
stay mainly in her yard
but one of them
landed on my car
snuck its small body
between the wiper
and the windshield,
discovered on the highway
translucent wings a wild flutter
holding onto glass in the wind.
Pulling off the first exit
the bee was gone
leaving a film of pollen
a bit of wing.

Flutter

Gone are the days
of bubble gum and bloody knees
the patter of feet on stairs,
the spilling over of bath water
high squeals and fighting words
battles for who was first
to the car, to the table
everything but to bed
the night time tears
that ended with a book
or a song, the long look
after my children slept
a wish to stop time's flutter
to let them be small a while.

Wave

this is a rogue wave
this is a violent song
big fish eat little fish
you can drown here
and I could let you

so easy to lose you
to the shark below
to the killer whale
you are my angel
I am your damselfish

we churn with the foam
splash our fins
spit out surf and grey salt
your waves meet mine
and tsunamis happen

this is a not a shipwreck
this is a powerful slap
a riptide surge filled
with bait and flotsam
a wall of water pounding sand

sometimes I hear the clock speak

a knock and sequence, hands
unsuccessful, reach for numbers

twelve hovers atop
a round white mountain

long sweeping curve of shrug
a gesture in one direction

the hiccup of a second
the thousand spins of a life.

LORI DESROSIERS is the author of *The Philosopher's Daughter*, published by Salmon Poetry in 2013 and a chapbook, *Inner Sky* from Glass Lyre Press. *Sometimes I Hear the Clock Speak* is her second full-length collection. Her poems have appeared in *New Millennium Review, Contemporary American Voices, Best Indie Lit New England, String Poet, Blue Fifth Review, Pirene's Fountain, The New Verse News, The Mom Egg, The Bloomsbury Anthology of Contemporary Jewish-American Poetry* and many other journals and anthologies. Her work has been nominated for a Pushcart Prize. She edits *Naugatuck River Review*, a journal of narrative poetry and *WORDPEACE*, an online journal dedicated to peace and justice. She teaches Literature and Composition at Westfield State University and Holyoke Community College, and Poetry in the Interdisciplinary Studies program for the Lesley University M.F.A. graduate program.